Published by Ricochet Editions
www.ricochetedeitions.com

ricochet

Ricochet Editions is an imprint of Gold Line Press, founded in 2012. Our mission is to publish innovative, non-traditional, trans-genre, or genre-less works that have a hard time finding homes in journals, competitions, and with other chapbook publishers. Ricochet is associated with the University of Southern California's Ph.D. program in Literature and Creative Writing.

Ricochet chapbooks are distributed by Small Press Distribution
www.spdbooks.org / 800-869-7553

This title is also available for purchase directly from the publisher

Book design by Scott Massey and Diana Arterian
Ricochet logo by Dylan Sung

Library of Congress Cataloging-in-Publication Data
Sutton Kiefer, Molly
Nestuary / Molly Sutton Kiefer

Library of Congress Control Number 2013947656

ISBN 9781938900051

9 8 7 6 5 4 3 2 1

FIRST EDITION

NESTUARY

MOLLY
SUTTON KIEFER

for Finnegan,
my boyfish, my warmest organ

And in memory of Jim
builder of nests, strongest of oaks

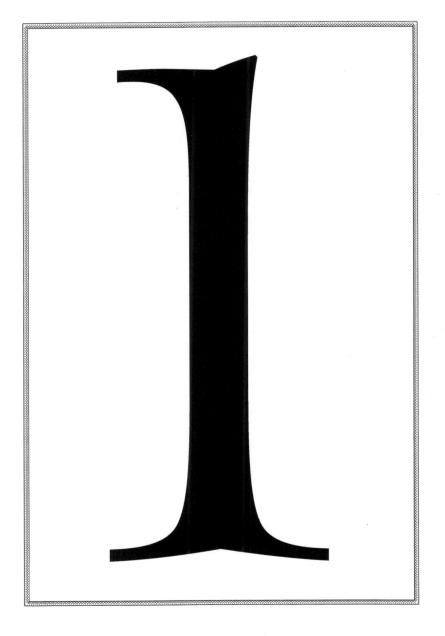

Each act of writing or mothering stuns by the immensity of its hidden archaeology of failure, riddled origins, hidden clauses, minute pleasures achieved through tactical approximations.

—

ERICA HUNT
"The World Is Not Precisely Round"
The Grand Permission

The ritual of drawing down the moon involves an invocation—that is, a welcoming of a goddess directly into the body.

Thessalian witches were believed to control the moon:

> *If I command the moon, it will come down; and if I wish to withhold the day, night will linger over my head; and again, if I wish to embark on the sea, I need no ship, and if I wish to fly through the air, I am free from my weight.*

Psychoanalyst Mel D. Farber explains this ceremony as linked to the protective-mother fantasy.

> *Wiccans say this ritual allows the priestess to become the Goddess on Earth. This experience can involve empowerment, healing from illness or injury, letting go of fear and accepting courage, releasing pessimism, relieving depression, & c. Each plucking. Finding a way to heal the body with the body.*

Among offerings, the invocation involves the following statement:

> *I am the Mother of all life, the One who watches over all. I am the wind in the sky, the spark in the fire, the*

seedling in the earth, the water in the river. I am the vessel from which All Things spring forth.

Clarity of intention is crucial.

Clarity of intention is cruel.

I imagine the night sky properly disrobed, leaving only the chips of light and blackest black. I imagine a woman in white swallowing the bulb of the moon, wearing it at her center.

I sing of questing, of bows-and-arrows, of Amazons with the mythic singular, of the truth of two and teats and sky clusters.

> *We look beyond clots of tree-and-snow to see what else forms.*

I armor, pull pinfeathers and boughs of pine and they become nest; I promise Hestia a clean kitchen, a bowl for yeast.

> *We herald the moon, each peach, the pit, touches the center of you.*

I yank at my hair and let those strands to the wind too: the birdwoman will braid them now, the tree's crook goldening.

> *We watch as she ties robin's eggs down, chips of sky. Twigs. More of the body.*

I sing in a place of me I did not know existed: the throat of me, the roar of wind, the tunnel to my bright stomach, kettledrum.

❀

i. A pregnancy is sometimes wished for. A half moon is what one becomes. Tools to use on the journey: thermometer, preferably the sort with an extra decibel; an instrument for writing, maybe in the sand; a chart, which can be found crumpled in a garbage bin. Flatten, try again. Measure oneself in the mornings, before hips have swung, feet spread. Find equilibrium in the sun-tones.

ii. In 1598, John Florio spent time with ink and quill, tapping housecat with nib; defined pregnancy *greatnes with child, pregnancie, a being great with childe or with yoong.* There was crooning, toms at the door. The housecat was nibbled. Nibbled back.

iii. My mother told me I was an easy pregnancy. She never threw up, and though she only menstruated once or twice a year (she had polycystic ovaries too), she formed me on the first try. Whose body is it? Acquiring my sister took three or four cycles, medicine bottles. She had been ready to give up, how long it was taking. My sister pinched at my mother's insides. Mother's legs don't show as much. Mine are covered in stretch stains.

iv. Suppose we all could feel a pregnancy simultaneously. Suppose my stomach were made of clear glass, a fish-bowl. I can hear it: you are wishing too. I would dictate the swish, that minnow-flick, know it: she's hiding.

My androgen levels are too high. This leads to these symptoms: weight gain, acne, hirsutism, diabetes (my test came back negative), patches and skin tags (not as far as I know), snoring (poor husband), depression or anxiety, and also the trouble ovulating. While there is no proof that polycystic ovary syndrome is genetic, research has shown that often women who have PCOS also have a mother who has had it (true, in my case) or a sister who has it (we don't know—she's on birth control and without the same generous coverage that I have; determining fertility is frivolous for her).

Women who have PCOS cannot make all the hormones the egg needs to fully mature. Follicles may start to grow and build up fluid. Some follicles may remain as cysts, and since no follicle becomes large enough and no egg matures or is released, ovulation does not occur and the hormone progesterone, which allows for regular menstruation, is absent. Additionally, the cysts develop male hormones, which also prevents ovulation.

I can tell you this (now): *This story has a happy ending.*

❀

LA LECHE
LEAGUE

Her name taken
for the prim group of women
hollowing a place at the dinner
                              table
little divots for milkpaws. It's made
for calls-in-the-night, sponsors,
and liquid shots.

In Florida,
she is Mother of Maternal Desires.
The desperate come and leave
little flags of want.

Try bending to your knees.
Wear it like an apron: desire.
Covet the chipped infant
in her arms.

PRAYER TO OUR
LADY OF LA LECHE

Lovely Lady of La Leche, most
loving Mother of our Savior, Jesus
Christ,
and my Mother, please listen
to my humble prayer. Your heart
knows my every wish, my every need.
I trust, dear Mother, that you will
shelter me beneath your protecting
mantle,
like what you did to your Son. Intercede
to Him that I may have the courage
and the strength to overcome
whatever difficulty surrounds me.
Give me the grace to be faithful
to you always and may you be
my shining inspiration now and forever.
Amen.

Perhaps it's that nothing went quite as planned. I was given the diagnosis of polycystic ovaries; I failed, and I fail, to ovulate.

> *You are meant to be a mother. Your body is designed for it. That is what this part of your body is for.*

I felt as if I were a pincushion: blood tests, samplings for glucose levels, pregnancy tests and slow measure of medicine, morning temperatures taken with one wand, my urine daily with another. There was the month I turned to acupuncture, stretched on my back, staring up at a rough-woven tapestry, my skin tingling at the site of perforation.

When I was pregnant, my fingers became pins, at least in the sense of tingling, and I would lumber to the bathroom with a mild form of hyperemesis—a semblance of oxymoron, of course, hyperemesis being *severe morning sickness*—and there was the threat of another needle in my arm, that of the IV to replace lost fluids. Instead, a daily purge and I'd toddle on. There was the restless legs syndrome, the odd feeling of bugs or lightning, in my elbow and shoulder, the bob in restaurants and constant insomnia.

I was a miserable pregnant woman, shocking my friends, who had pictured me as an Earth Mama, and told me so. Barefoot and fat and happy. My body was all wrong.

❈

The appointments, the discovery, came about because I didn't want to menstruate on my honeymoon. A friend had done the same a few months previous: the luxury of not bleeding on a beach. I shivered at this control of her body; I wanted nature to do it for me. But that loomingness: *What's a honeymoon for*?

Then, children were far from my mind. Just the growing old with someone.

The bleeding didn't come. For the first time in my life, I began to track, ticks on a calendar, and one month, and another, and the honeymoon passed and another month stumbled into another month and then I was in the doctor's office. And she was sweeping her hand against her jawline, asking me about the pecking order of my parts, and I felt the hot flush of shame. Yes, yes, yes, and there it was, a packaged pill.

A woman's hormones spin out of control. (This might be hyperbole.) What I mean is, one's hormones cause one's bleedings to stop, no longer in obedience to the moon. Ovulation simply halts.

What I mean is this could lead to heart disease, diabetes. If left alone, missing one's cycles in such a vagrant state could lead to endometrial cancer.

Too, there is the clump of physical altercations. Insult to injury.

Even as a teenager, my acne was not so virulent.

> *You have a zit.*
> It glares back, puffed up & angry.

I had once been made of sticks, light me like tinder. Slender and lovely, little arms wrapped around little knees.

PCOS gives you a barrel quality, abdominal drum. Waddling before the product.

Strangely enough, while exercise is recommended, the system confuses, panics, gathers mob mentality. Women with PCOS are generally insulin resistant.

> *Those shoes make you look fatter than you actually are.*

Hair too. Little witchy chin-hairs, sprung black strands around my belly button. In the bath, I watch them wave.

Moon, I'm hollowing toward you,
funneling into air. My skin
is plucked like yours,
the O-rose of your mouth—

I knew there was something a little askew about my body: the first time I took a pregnancy test was a decade ago. I crept down the pharmacy aisles, tucked a pink box into my armpit.

My best friend knew to the hour when her blood would begin. Me, I would come home in a panic, frantically changing underwear, cursing the cramp and press, the unpredictability of my cycle.

Even on medication, my period would stray. I found my medicine cabinet stocked with pregnancy tests—just in case. I'd hide them beneath towels, afraid my husband would tell me to stop wasting money.

Not long after my friend took her one and only pregnancy test, I was assigned the task of accompanying her to breast-feeding class. Her husband, dutiful in all other coursework, bowed out of the milkshot one. She and I had a tan baby with dead eyes. I picked up on the dynamics of football hold before she did.

At the birth, I was the third person in the room. I watched her strip to clung shirt and underwear, watched her sink into the whirlpool, her breasts filming. When my god-son disembarked, I held his mother's left foot. His skull cross-hatched. My own eyes bulged *heisdying heisdying whyisnoonedoinganything.* I didn't know of cranial molds and cranial sutures. How was I to know?

The doctor snipped her and the baby came out in a rush of shit and blood and suddenly was squalling, on her chest, squalling.

fig 1. At an exhibition, I was able to peer into the canyon of the dead woman's body. This woman stands erect, skin peeled back, organs pulled away to reveal: ovary, fallopian tube, uterus. All without anything to say.

fig 2. I think of all the tumors with spindles of hair, clutches of teeth. Mine is a smooth pearled problem. In the glass case is a cystic self, but how to discern invasion from welcomed growth—mirroring healthy, smooth-walled, obstructive.

fig 1. Sinew is heat lightning across her cheeks. The hearty spin and curl of intestines thrust out. Glands are clamshells adorning her throat. Smooth shouldered strokes of muscle. Nose-shaped ovary, knob of flesh. Drape of omentum. Primate ears, flared nostrils. Round sponge of petite breasts. Wrinkled flesh, button-badge nipples.

fig 2. Peach pit: wrinkled and old and all that's left over. A little meat there. It's an object I can carry by marsupial pouch, keep it with me every day, reach down and touch it— *touch it*—lines and caverns and shape of something—not empty but not becoming.

⽊

In wanting this, I pit myself against myself.

The Roman goddess Diana causes me to catch my breath.

She is: the goddess of the hunt, the moon, and birthing. She is rooted in the oak groves; her midwife is a water nymph.

Her name is dewy on my lips.

A cult formed around Diana; women would pray to become pregnant and once pregnant, pray for an easy delivery.

Diana and the companions she kept were all virgins.

Take two branches and bow. These are the chambers of the quickening heart.

❀

I could have said: *No, I'm not, I can prove it by all those negative plastic pregnancy wands, all those no's, one right after another.*

My regimen reveals it wasn't for lack of effort; some days I was on as many as ten pills a day. Lexapro for the anxiety disorder; everything else, though, is for that four-letter word—*baby*: a prenatal vitamin; one Provera to encourage the monthly bleed; Clomid, which stimulates ovulation; the fish oil to lower the cholesterol that raised because of the PCOS; and four-a-day of Metformin, which does something with insulin, and had me sprinting for the bathroom much of Thanksgiving Day. During the preparation of the meal, I abandoned my fraught husband four times, once to throw up in the bathroom sink.

Later, I'd quietly give thanks: for knowing, for insurance, for him.

But no. Thanks for asking, I'm *not* pregnant.

Really.

My month does not follow the Gregorian calendar—my body dictates the numbers. In the months that we attempted to have a baby, my body arbitrated the following: day one is now the first day of menstruation; days five through nine are for the Clomid doses; then there's days eleven through eighteen, which are supposed to be *fun*, but mostly involve wheedling my husband and reminding him of the limits of insurance and the costs of infertility treatments; day twenty-three is when my blood is drawn to see if the Clomid did its job; twenty-eight is the pregnancy test day, though if you are anything like me, you've probably taken half a dozen along the way, *just in case*, a kick of disappointment each time. *No, certainly not, not the least bit pregnant.*

My condition also allows for two monthly trips to the doctor. At first indication of non-pregnancy, a failed month, I make an ultrasound appointment, which ideally must occur before the Clomid cycle. It is to make certain I have no cysts on my ovaries, because the Clomid is a stimulant and one does not want to stimulate those sacs of fluid.

This is done with my ass out, my tail in the breeze, and this ultrasound is not up-top, not the deodorant-stick sized creature that, a few years prior, checked my breast lump, but instead something resembling a probe, something she moves within me like a gear shift, aggressively searching for my second, more timid ovary, checking for cysts, scattered peas.

The first visit was done in eerie-silence, the sound of machinery-buzz and my worry filling the room. The second involves chatter. She's already pointed out my bladder and dark marks she explains are fecal matter.

I have what's she's called a *shy ovary*, one that tends to hide. The first time it was tucked in the folds of my organs and such; the second, she's decided, is mimicking and hiding with the first. She tries the abdominal ultrasound to make certain, pressing into my bladder, leaving a slug-trail of lubricant. Instead of a baby, the offending ovary glares back.

She explains ovary stimulation, teasing of the low possibility of having a litter, and always leaves on an optimistic note, saying she the next time she sees me, she hopes it will be a prenatal check-up.

We'll have you take a pregnancy test before you leave.

She doesn't know how cruel it is to give that anticipation. I am ruined at the repeated instances of *no*—a negative progesterone test for ovulation, four peed-upon plastic sticks, once more into a cup, as if no one else believed me, especially not myself—

Not this time, darling, it didn't work out after all.
Let's begin again as we did before.
Let's find ourselves stripped at the waist.

✿

THE DOCTOR LEAVES MESSAGES

VOICEMAIL ONE.

I don't know what is beneath you now. The place where your body meets, first hemisphere and second, has found ways to pause. Think of soap bubbles. These are your ovaries. Each glissando, a cystic song. Beat those drums, the skin's come loose! We'll give you pills to prompt, diminutive stars that will burn, die out. You'll find your body beating against the ocean again, tide pulled by the moon. It will find you, lashed against the current.

VOICEMAIL TWO.

You've played Chutes and Ladders. (*It's not a question.*) You have a rain barrel, a cellar door. You will trace your fingers, each square a project, a string of satellites pressed against the ceiling. Place an hourglass next to your thermometer next to your nighttime reading. You have forty-eight hours before the roe will break.

VOICEMAIL THREE.

We know there are expectations, but the world is full of that half-slash *no*. Your uterus pipes that up, belly-organ, soft wheezes to balance the short burst of *no*. We want you back anyway, we love the table squirm—you do it so well.

VOICEMAIL FOUR.

Your body carved of stone, your convex mirror. Inside of you is a cave, lonely. Sometimes, when we come to a close, there is an echo, as if nothing happened at all. Ping of pellet against flesh-wall and flesh-wall singing back, dull hum to the edge of the world.

I am wicked to my body.

I lean into the mirror sometimes and say, *1 hate you 1 hate you 1hateyou.*

[**fol**-i-*kuh*l]

n.   doctor tells patient, pointing to the screen: chocolate chips in a cookie

adj.   this seems too domestic

n.   distended with air, elongated capsules

n.   a crypt; a cul-de-sac or lacuna

n.   botany: a dry seed pod, splitting at maturity only along the front of the suture, as in larkspur or milkweed

n.   a crypt; a cul-de-sac or lacuna

v.   altered: two centimeters or more and it morphs in name; see cyst

Origin: a shell, a bag, a day at the beach. A ship passing into port, a barrel of wine, an elongated telescope, a shoulder, a name whispered into the night.

[**met-fȯr-mən**]

v.   an act of shame, hovering in the bathroom, tilt-hustle down the corridor

n.   —you—round—four—moons

v.   listen: hear its path across the expanse, hollow field, comfort of blood vessel

n.   white chalk, applesauce on my tongue

v.   relinquish: bowels, routine, feel the cool of bathroom tile, feel the way the floor moves when the door opens

[**sist**]

adj.   the palm-up *no*, what is marked enemy

n.   *zoology*: sac surrounding an animal that has passed into dormant condition

v.   I sleep for hours after the appointments, think of winter

v.   response to extreme conditions; fall to lake bottom, remain quiescent for years

v.   I lumber, eat honey, am imaginary.

🐾

My friend travels on a grant to Japan in order to study preserved tattooed skin. She returns with a red ball in the palm of her hand: a Daruma, a gift for me.

Legend has it Bodhidharma was a Buddhist monk who meditated facing a wall for nine years without moving. His legs fell off from lack of movement. Another legend tells it this way: he fell asleep during his nine-year stretch and cut his eyelids away in anger.

The Daruma stares at me from his post on my bookshelf, eerie and angry. He's red-hooded with a golden swish on his front. White-eyed.

He's meant to be a charm, a totem, a piece of luck: yolk one eye in to make the wish, yolk the other when the wish comes true.

I have never been so cautious in coloring before. My fingers smell of Sharpie from the slowness, seeping into my fingertips, stretching into the brochioles of my lungs, and into the sideshow of my brain.

☙

I am a feral tomb.

"Like a dead woman I walk the fields in the tall grass, stalks of green light: I am Diana, the Huntress of gold, and I find only boneyards: I live in a stratum underlying feeling: I'm barely living."

I growl, in and out, like the breath.

"It's a tangled world of vines, syllables, honeysuckle, color, and words—the threshold of an ancestral cavern which is the uterus of the world, and from it shall I be born."

We lean into the trench.

❀

The winter we are trying, primetime television introduces two infertility narratives for the characters of their show. These arcs barely brush more than an episode or two and without treatment, both women, one of whom is a doctor, the other a lawyer, opt for adoption.

Women who could afford such a thing. We had made our charts, realizing we couldn't move beyond insurance's generous six-cycle limit, certainly couldn't afford the tens of thousands it would cost to adopt. We were growing old.

A narrative that takes up much more space, involves more characters, and thus, is much more interesting. No one desires to see a woman conveyer, for any amount of time.

Two days before my first son was born, I broke out in a rash which was tentatively diagnosed as measles, and was admitted to a hospital for contagious diseases to await the onset of labor. I felt for the first time a great deal of conscious fear, and guilt toward my unborn child, for having 'failed' him with my body in this way.

—

ADRIENNE RICH
Of Woman Born

We travel to Denver, Colorado with friends.

Fingers clench winged muscles.

My health insurance as a graduate instructor covers six cycles, regardless of specifics.

We lap at the coves of one another.

We are on our fifth.

I touch the cord of your neck.

Our friends are always here. We love them, but they are *always fucking here.*

Our bodies hum and hum against one another.

I beg him to go into the bathroom with me. Hop up on the edge of the shower. *Anything.*

Your body is a hook.

Nothing. We drive back to Minnesota, overnight, get to our house at six in the morning. He plans to sleep for an hour, go in to work. I tell him he can sleep in just a moment.

We tilt and tip the bed.

This is The Cycle That Wasn't Meant To Be. I thought it was too late.

After, all I smell is the musk of us.

And yet it was the cycle that was.

I'm remarkably and unsurprisingly *baδ* at being pregnant. I collect these foibles, stones in my pocket:

1   Before I even know I am pregnant, I begin to suck at the cave of my mouth: excess saliva an indication of things to come. Evidence of hormonal-shifts (*I envisioneδ tectonic plates*) and the hesitancy to swallow, the onset of nausea (*great oceans sloshing*).

2   Then the yes, then the groove I made, knitting slipper to carpet, how I learned to not rush. I could hold bile in the palm of my torso, and I could even tell it to *just wait* while I finished a chapter, because it wasn't like the stomach flu where one is all wings and flurried paper, dust and a chronicle of speed. No, this was sluggish, but it was relentless. Every living day I was there, telling the toilet the same story, over and over, it became a routine, like how high school teachers eventually control their bowels to offload during prep hour; I remember how my stolen hour was switched from second to fifth period and my body was so angry and *wouldn't change* so I had to slip out during small group work and they must have thought I had a real problem but honestly, when your digestion is regulated into

blocks of time like that, all it can do is follow instructions, wear a groove.

3   The nausea seemed separate, somehow. My reflex was to recoil from ginger. Fennel, lavender, thyme. I wore seasickness bands that simply looked like my way of drawing myself back into the 80s. I wasn't fond of tea. B6 changed nothing. Small curbings: lemon water, watermelon-flavored hard candy.

4   Slender pain started in my wrists. Slow tingle. It started when I was knitting a kicking bag for the baby. A cabled sleeping sack. Little strands of sock yarn tangled at my feet. It started with one wrist guard, then another. It started with one brand, tan-colored to blend with my skin. I learned to write clearly with curved metal shafts abutting my thumb. I wore black wristguards, which began to smell like vinegar from my sweat. I wore them in class, then while driving, then while awake, then while asleep, until the only time I gave them respite was when I showered. Even then, my hands tingled, grew numb.

5   I developed restless legs syndrome, which isn't, as I had thought, simply overly-caffeinated knees

bouncing in a conference room. It was, instead, a very serious neurological disease, also called Willis-Ekbom Disease. For me, it felt as if a feather were stroking the confines of my knee, my hip, my shoulder. All on the left side. At dinner in an Italian restaurant, I shrugged my shoulders out of tempo, my father chiding me. If I didn't move, the feather would continue its slow revolving, driving me mad.

6 Serotonin levels skidded. Already steeped in depression and anxiety, these heightened. I sat in my Epic in Translation course and felt my chest squeeze shut. Winter in Minnesota is always night.

I would tell myself: each thing will make her stronger. Each thing will keep her safe.

❀

Head over toilet; this is a new view, the spur on a stick.
I find myself this way over and over:
kneeling at garden's edge, seedlings wilting as I wait,
breath caught, my own mournful merchandise.

SOMETIMES WITH RLS: A FANTASY

1 Have you—lately—danced the jitterbug? I'll hip around you: *lean in.*

2 Sliver hangnail moon. My bending parts treadle the night floor.

3 Reckless conga with the banister. Have you ever kissed a tumbleweed?

4 I want to hope before the birds come out. Hop a skiff. Don a pope.

5 Pillow-ruined eyes. Let the bones collapse on themselves.

6 Unstitch the fire, little burrs of flame. Ravish the sun.

7 I'll switch all the off-and-on-ramps. No scurry will notice.

8 Little tethers balloon like an argument.

9 Ice cream-scoop out a hollow. Nary a joint left. Jettison the stone.

One of Heracles' many labors was to destroy the hydra. For every of its nine serpent heads he decapitated, two more would spring forth. The only way he could prevent this regeneration was to cauterize the wounds.

—

Why are there so many images of the headless pregnant woman? Even those so-called self portraits, the *selfies* (as if we were bucketing over and giving ourselves pleasure) in the mirror. And elsewhere, the advertisements to the torso.

—

A collection of headless portraits from the Victorian Era have gone viral on social media. Some of the photographers used a collage method: cutting the image, reassembling, re-photographing. The more expert images likely used a blocking technique with a carefully shaped matte and reverse matte with two photos on the same photographic paper. The photographer would need to shift the mattes slightly, similar to dodging and burning, in order to blend the two originals together. Two women pose in conversation, one woman holding another's smiling head in her palm. Two adolescents give steely gaze to the camera, the girl holding a hatchet, the boy holding his mother's head. Her neckstem shows through the ruffles of her dress.

Beth Ann Fennelly tells her former student in a letter:

> I think our inability to recall and relive the memory of the pain has to do with the fact that during hard labor, you go to a place beyond language. It isn't so much that there are no good words to describe what you're going through as that there are no words. Margaret Atwood captures this beautifully in her short story "Giving Birth." Atwood's narrator is advised to take an epidural so she doesn't have to go through pain. "She thinks, *What pain?*... When there is no pain she feels nothing, when there is pain, she feels nothing because there is no she." We use the word "disembodied" a lot, but truly it applies here because the body breaks free from the ego.

I am rooted into my body. I have oak leaves growing in my hair. I am every piece of me.

1988   Victoria Campos was shot in the head. She was twenty-four years old. The wound to her right temple was allegedly inflicted by her husband on New Year's Eve. She was reportedly kept alive on a ventilator to deliver a more mature baby.

1999   In December, a woman named Milagros, which means *miracles*, was put on life support. She was thirty-four years old. Her heart stopped beating after a failed operation. She was a homeless heroin addict and had lost contact with most of her family. Before heart surgery, she was told by her doctors that aborting the baby could save her life. Her baby was born at twenty-six weeks. Many spoke out about the Catholic belief that the "sinful" mother is less valued than the innocent child.

2005   Sarah M. Fay was attacked on the Big Island of Hawai'i. She was thirty-four years old. She was seven weeks pregnant with her boyfriend Marwann Timothy Saad Jackson's child. Jackson was charged with murder in connection with her beating—the police stated she was "declared dead as a matter of law." Jackson's criminal record contained eighteen prior charges, including striking another man with a coconut, causing a gash. Her sister blamed Sarah's "traumatic bond" with her killer; she also reported her sister would be taken off life support after the baby was born "so that she can rest peacefully."

2005   Susan Torres lost consciousness at the dinner table. She was twenty-six years old. She had had a stroke, which was caused by a brain tumor, which was caused by the melanoma she had when she was seventeen, which had returned. She was seventeen weeks pregnant at the time. She was kept on life support in order to deliver a more viable baby; her husband confessed, "I hate using her as a husk, a carrying case." Ten weeks later, baby Susan was born at one pound, thirteen ounces. The baby died a little over a month later, after surgery for a perforated intestine.

2006   Veronica Celis was brain-dead from cancer. She was thirty-six years old. The doctors wanted to wait until she was thirty-two weeks along, but a bacterial infection began to spread. Her daughter was born weighing two pounds, fifteen ounces. After baby Veronica was born, she was placed at her mother's side, and her father pressed his lips to one, then the other. The mother was taken off life support the next day; the father did not want his child to share a birthday with her mother's death day.

2012   In April, Christine Bolden collapsed in a parking lot. She was twenty-six years old. She suffered two brain aneurysms. She was kept on a respirator for a month, and her twin sons were born at twenty-five weeks.

❁

Not long after I meet my husband, we go to a place in the middle of the Wisconsin woods, near abandoned train tracks, a bridge fallen into a gorge, where we watch a meteor shower. Months later, we are drawn to the side of the road and watch the Aurora Borealis. We are nineteen. We are twenty.

—

The Pleiades is an open star cluster and can be seen in the winter sky by the naked eye. These stars are named for the seven daughters of the Titan Atlas and the sea-nymph Pleione. The Greek myth tells of how the sisters are pursued by a giant huntsman and are turned into doves for safe keeping. Another narrative has the daughters mourning Atlas's humiliation and slipping into dove-form to save their father any further embarrassment. Maia couples with Zeus and forms Hermes.

Maia. The month of May. The Maker. May Day.

We name our daughter Maya, the Greco-Roman goddess of the earth.

Not long before I gave birth to my daughter, I read an article called "Encouraging Words, Unintentional Harm" in a holistic magazine. As the article digs in, the authors state, "Some quotes, if misread, serve to place birth as a competitive act, pitting women against each other. Others appear to point the finger at the woman herself as being to blame for a less-than great birth."

This is in reference to a quote meant to empower: *There is a secret in our culture, and it is not that birth is painful, but that women are strong.* It's likely intended in the Hallmark/refrigerator-magnet sort of way, a talisman worn from a cord at the throat, whanging against the belly, reminding the self with each dedicated step: *strong, strong, strong.* The implication, then, is that if you have a traumatic birth, you often feel you were not *strong enough*, when often it's really that one ought to feel *safe enough*.

Kettle-lit: how to make music from this deep place? Each divot, a new tone, a sweet song. I hold her, my papaya, in my deepest drum.

In the autumn before Maya is born, my yoga instructor has her pregnant students select a word—a word that could become a mantra in the birthing room. Most of the women around me are hoping for a natural birth, as am I, and they plan to surround themselves with support—midwives, doulas, a water birth, calming music. They said: *courage, peace, no drugs!* When it came time for me to pick a word, I claim *open*. I want to close my eyes and urge my body to open up, to feel that light within as she enters the world.

My husband and I whittle away our last days watching Discovery Channel and indulge in *Gold Rush*, a show about mining in Alaska. In it, a white-bearded chipmunk of a man hops around, chittering about a glory hole.

In gold mining, this often is an eroded depression at the base of an ancient waterfall, usually containing large deposits of gold.

In glassblowing, the glory hole is one of the furnaces used to reheat the glass while shaping it. The tip of the blow-pipe is inserted and rotated, glass gathered like honey on a dipper.

I decide, in my hormonal stupor, to nickname my vagina-as-birthing-object my "glory hole."

Later I learn the grittier usage of glory hole: a hip-high hole in a partition between bathroom stalls in which to experience anonymous sexual encounters. I think of chaffing and duct tape and unknowing.

When telling a friend about this passage, she tells me of the grey-haired barista whose name is Gloria Hole. I tell her the chipmunk's name is Jack Hoffman.

PLEASE INDICATE WHICH OPTIONS YOU WOULD PREFER
DURING YOUR BIRTHING EXPERIENCE.

1   Wet, wet. Yearning swirl of bathwater and float. Your partner's hand can press down, keep you from overflowing.

2   The audience with applause sign. It is how we cheer you on.

3   No salt on the wound. No oils, no ointments, no scents of any sort.

4   There is: wheelbarrow, monkey-squat, draw your finger through the dust, ankle clasping, treble clef.

5   Peel away. Assurances through soft music. Ocean waves optional.

6   The distribution of popcorn is not required, though menu choices are slim. The viewing begins in a few hours, and this machine becomes the central line.

7   Blackened windows can be your mirror. Do not inspect below the belt line.

8   Little needle song.

9   Hypnotic breathing. Pufferfish have a pelagic life stage. Spawning occurs near surface; eggs are spherical and buoyant. Keep you from overflowing.

10 Please place the creature on my chest. Please let the broth of me slick away.

11 Please sing humble songs of needles and knives and everything that shines.

❀

Diana's Greek equivalent is Artemis. Among her virgin hunting companions was the nymph Callisto. She was seduced by Zeus-in-disguise and became great with child, a vast offense among the huntresses. Artemis transformed the offending Callisto into a bear—though some would have it the jealous wife Hera did this deed—and to protect her, the bear was cast among stars, becoming Ursa Major.

This star sequence, brightest in April, can be seen throughout the year in the northern hemisphere. Its brightest stars make up those of the Big Dipper.

—

Some studies have performed the *sonification of light curves*. The sound of the stars. The studies involve frequencies of brightness and can be listened to on Internet databases. Rumor has it that a star being consumed sounds like a D-sharp played well below the range of the human ear.

—

Women who shriek during birth often have a harder time than those who learn to groan, deep within the body. This vibration is soothing. They call this practice *sounding the birth*. This is what I do while staring at a pastel painting of a water bridge as contraction after contraction lights up the night sky.

❀

Forty-two hours after my first contraction, my body, indeed, *did* open: my daughter was born through a slit in my abdomen and into the fluorescent light of the operating room.

I had gotten through four nurses' shifts (they come on in twelve-hour spreads) and two doctors' (twenty-four hour) shifts. The anesthetist spent FORTY-FIVE minutes attempting an epidural, each moment fully felt, contracted through—even the rope of blood that slipped down my back, I felt that too, the clinch of my husband's hands bearing down, holding me in place.

I imagined him sweating and wanting to swear. The anesthetist. And my husband.

I wanted to be on all fours, huffing. I wanted to squat on the floor as if I were about to shit out my baby. I wanted my body to animal, me to howl. Howling got me through the first day. But.

I had waited over twenty-four hours for any pain medication—waited, no *denied*—no, nurse; no, company; no, self—but after a forty-five minute sequence of unrelenting contractions, a sequence that felt like one—very— l/o/n/g—contraction, I gave in. I gave in and gave in.

The bullying woman who "delivered" me had pressed these words on me, twelve hours before it happened, a threat in the air: *Cesarean section.* I would have folded at first suggestion, had it not be for the providence of having my partner, defending my birth plan, asking for more time.

In Sharon Olds' silver-screened poem "I Go Back To May 1937," she closes the poems with these searing words: "Do what you are going to do, and I will tell about it." Perhaps this became my new mantra, the something I whispered in my head to the bulldogged doctor, forgiving and ruining her for it.

On the form I needed to sign, the one pardoning all for the trauma before and any to come, this was written as the reason for the C-section: *failure to progress.* My body had begun to swell shut.

It should come as no great surprise that my nightstand was cluttered with pregnancy guides. I read the same story, month-by-month, over and over. Little nugget of flesh, fleshing.

The thing is: I skipped the chapters on C-sections.

And this too: the night of the class on C-sections, it was snowing. We stayed home.

My mother had a long labor with me. Longish. Twenty-four hours, and I would joke as a teenager about how I was difficult from the start. But I sprung forth, from her glory hole. None of my friends had C-sections.

Nothing by way of example, which meant it couldn't happen to me.

For the record.

The story that Julius Caesar was born via Caesarean section is false. C-sections were performed in Roman times, but there is no documentation of a mother surviving one. Instead, C-sections were only permitted when the mother died (or was dying) during childbirth. Caesar's mother Aurelia is reputed to have survived her son's birth.

It is also suspected the term is derived from the verb *caedere,* which means *to cut,* as in *cut from the womb.*

In some translations, Caesarean section means *emperor's cut, emperor incision, imperial cut, tzar cut.*

In Greek mythology, Apollo removed Asclepius, his son (and eventual god of medicine and ancient healing) from his mother's abdomen. In one version, Apollo casts Asclepius's mother Coronis into a fire, and Asclepius is drawn from his mother's corpse.

❀

In Shakespeare's *Macbeth*, the power-hungry title character visits three witches, clanging a cauldron, generally staged in a cave. Wombs within wombs. Thunder and incantation.

Macbeth is visited by apparitions, and the second is a wounded child, who tells:

> *Be bloody, bold, and resolute; laugh to scorn*
> *The power of man, for none of woman born*
> *Shall harm Macbeth.*

What a blessed relief! This isn't a possibility, particularly since the first apparition warned to *Beware Macduff*. No one but a monster could not be of woman born. Something sprung from a forehead. A sea creature, an egged wonder. But—

> *Despair they charm,*
> *And let the angel whom thou still has served*
> *Tell thee, Macduff was from his mother's womb*
> *Untimely ripp'd.*

A riddle resolved, but not a mother. Gutted like a fish, seam-torn, this mother is left to waste.

Some say the rip negates the more gentle Caesarian section. *Not born but torn.*

This begs the question: did I *give* birth? Isn't *giving* active? My body was numbed like a winter-frozen carrot. I did no pushing, so then did the doctor *birth*? She reached in, drew my daughter's blood-slick body into the wild light of the operating room.

Gutted like a fish, unsprung, unstirred from my cauldron.

Failure begets shame, a kind of powerful, pumping horror. I needed hope, curled against me.

Camille Roy writes, "The relation of baby to body will be ripped apart and then organized by shame."

Toi Derricotte writes, "I couldn't tell where my shame ended and his life began. It was as if my body betrayed me, became evidence against me."

I felt I had wronged her, somehow. This wasn't supposed to be our story, was it?

As I read, post-birth, swaddled in absorbent pads that could engulf my newborn's diapers, my body weeping with fluids, the doctor pushing a cotton swab into my deeply infected Cesarean scar, I discovered I wasn't alone.

Gillian Conoley told it first: "My labor was horrendous— six days of contractions, four days of intensive labor— back labor, predromal labor, a cervix that preferred to stay clinched like a fist rather than, as the midwives softly and irritatingly urged, 'opening like a rose.'"

I felt it in my chest, Naomi Wolf's description of her own traumatic birth experience: "I had now been flat on my side, scared, for an hour or so, without 'making progress,' as they put it. They kept saying the words, 'no progress' or 'failure to progress' and 'fetal distress,' a terrifying combination. No medical staffer that I can remember said 'You can do this.' I learned later the powerful physical effect words can have on a laboring woman."

I needed hope, not more slender needles.

❀

My child, I held her there, inside of me, *of my body*, which was a failure, in so many layered and evidenced ways. It was in the paper record now.

I remember when we were still trying and how I evaded the door of a car when it hurtled toward my stomach; my body already knew the instinct of the dodge as protection. Snarl and feral haunt.

Two years later, I am pushing my daughter in a stroller down the sidewalk and a car's lights seem to point too close; I am not thinking—I feel my body hula in the exact same trajectory.

It beats this way, *it knows*. But it is told, again and again what a failure it has become.

If it is introduced as merely a pin, it roots there, becomes a haystack of pins. One cannot search without bleeding.

❀

And still, Caroline cried, and Martha's nerves vibrated in extraordinary response, as if the child were connected to her flesh by innumerable invisible fibers.

—

DORIS LESSING
A Proper Marriage

Sharon Olds writes in *The Language of the Brag*: "I have done this thing, / I and the other women this exceptional / act with the exceptional heroic body, / this giving birth, this glistening verb."

My body halved on that table, my self doubled.

It isn't the birth that is the hero of this story. The cause for physical triumph is instead the nesting-in, hiding-beneath-a-blanket-of-snow. I held her within long enough, and then I held her again without.

My verb came in brilliant spurts of blue-white. I'd indicate my floppy chest, crow a bit.

The snow waked against our windows; it was only Me and Her.

Naomi Wolf writes, "By the time she had found my breast and clung to me like a shipwrecked traveler, I was entirely hers."

We nestled in, we shipped, we rode that blue sea. We rafted on pillows, and I wrote about it. We were mapping the body and its new workings.

My body hadn't known this want. The ache and release. The satisfaction of nipple and tongue.

Leslie Adrienne Miller, in "To Make A Wound," writes, "He can't resist the cheek that speaks of sea / spray, tastes of fleece, milk and pearl. / He hasn't even discovered my boy's chubby toes and soft hip handles, / his creamy bracelets of pulp."

Is it permissible to swallow your daughter's limbs? I want to wallow them into my maw like a fish, *sluuuuuurp*. I want to feel her little thighs vibrate against the pulp of my mouth.

Fennelly: "The erotics of motherhood—in our culture it's taboo... the teardrop glottis at the back of their throats vibrating with anger and hunger while you're fumbling with the buttons of your blouse, then your nursing bra, and your breasts feel the surge of warm milk rushing to the ducts, and finally the child has at it, the braided sweet river is sluicing down her tongue, she is drifting the boat of your arms with her tiny fingers over the side, rippling the water."

I press my nose to her skin and breathe. And breathe.

❀

I grew up with Bible excerpts and Shakespeare, retold by my father, as bedtime and bathtime stories. I knew of the flood, Romeo and Juliet's melodrama, Abraham's faith, Daniel and Jonah and David, fairies and forests. I was fascinated when he'd dramatically tell me about the monkey's paw, his eyes a bit bulgy, his knuckles rapping on the wood- paneled walls.

I remember clearly the swing he and my mother tethered to a pine in our backyard. I remember fluffing up piles of needles to leap into, how high and thick they went, how garden snakes made homes there. I remember the sun beating through pockets in the tree as I lifted my legs in and wafted the air, my father telling me the story of Solomon: the two women, one childless, snarling over the same baby, the offering of division, the "real" mother sacrificing her life so that the child may live.

I married into a Catholic family; his parents are often Eucharistic ministers. I know this involves administering the bread and wine, and at the close of communion, the wine must be finished. My mother-in-law doesn't drink much, so she gives her husband that duty. She jokes about tipping down the church stairs.

> *transubstantiation*: the miraculous change by which according to Roman Catholic and Eastern

Orthodox dogma the Eucharistic elements at their consecration become the body and blood of Christ while keeping only the appearances of bread and wine

transmogrify: (trans v.) to change or alter greatly and often with grotesque or humorous effect

In some churches, when giving the host, the priest says, *This is my body, given for you.*

Because of the growling sound she makes while nursing, I call her The Bear.

Others pick it up: my mother knits her a costume for Halloween, with pink ears and wispy yarn; my husband calls her Maya-Bear when he lifts her into his arms.

Her first animal-sound is a roar, which we do in swimming lessons, my legs bouncing, her roar bouncing from tile to tile. She is magnificent.

[**nest**]

adj.   pocketlike, holder of little blonde eggs

n.   the make of sticks, of feathers-from-your-hair, brittle last-year's leaves

v.   bottoming out, carrying, belly-to-belly and fleshed

adj.   that secret pleasure of down, windy eggs

n.   a home for toys, as in *nesting dolls*, the center a prize, *pling!*

v.   deposit some treasure

[**hahrth**]

n   the place we warm within the nest

adj   a lisping, as in *I love you with all my hearth*

v   *Metallurgy*: lowerings of a blast furnace, copola. Moltan. Metal. Pours out.

[**es**-choo-er-ee]

adj.   lit foam, snort and shuffle of fish blessings

v.   mouth meets the bray of tide

v.   where milk clevers its way from alveoli cells
to ductule to sinus to duct

n.   becoming the duck that swims within

[**sangk**-choo-er-ee]

n.   immunity from arrest; a translucent tissue

v.   Quasimodo, repugnant body, carried the street
dancer within

❀

Before babies, before graduate studies in poetry, before even marriage, I taught high school in a just-unwrapped, brand-new building. I stood in front of clusters of fourteen-year-old boys and spit and exasperated girls and dog collars and violent video games and telling them about Homer and host-guest behavior. It was a popped-up suburb, right where farm fields were tilled and those carbon copy mansions hunched on little plots of land.

And that year they voted against school funding because their mansions were empty of furniture and they'd already built this beautiful school with polished bricks and flat roofs. No place for songbirds nesting. So when they budget cut my ass, I threw a pomegranate, its electric juices staining our cheap wood floor and began my season of hyperventilating.

My lungs were two sodden rags. I'd face the wall and try to fill them to the bottom, that pit near my stomach, *let them touch*, and I couldn't do it. I'd make a noise: *heap, heap, heap.*

I wept through my annual physical that year. The doctor's voice strung itself along lungspace, edged in, some red dye, and I was soothed, as if my mother had rubbed my back and given me ice cream. During the exam, her fingers pressing, unpressing, pressing, unpressing, she found a lump. Two fingers, punching dough. I'd seek it at night, rub the marble under my flesh.

I was given an ultrasound, then a biopsy. My husband— no, then, fiancé—came and sat in a plastic chair on the other side of the curtain. I told him I'd wear the purple patient gown to our wedding that summer. Fetching! The little needle snapped at the lump, drawing out two squiggles of tissue. Later found to be a fibroadenoma. Harmless little lump.

I had two choices: I could have it removed, or I could monitor it and leave it be.

I kept it, little talisman. I wanted to remember this.

Bologna, Italy: Piazza Maggiore has a fountain dedicated to Neptune and the lactating mermaids. Fontana di Nettuno. The nymphs cup their breasts and pebbles of water curl out in varying directions. The water seems to shatter the air.

I do this in the shower when I am especially engorged, milking myself, pressing my thumb above the nipple to see how high the spray will go. I could make a wonderful water gun. I could write my name in the snow, the names of my children, my children's children.

It's true; I am one of those mermaids. I let in Hera who suckled Hercules, whose tear at her teat created the Milky Way.

❀

I begin to keep the milk, bags of it.

I stay-at-home. I do not need an extra ten ounces a day; other mothers balk at the excess. Some days I carry an extra pint in me. I let down in the bathtub, so I pull, long strokes, watch milk resemble smoke huffing from my nipples, become hydrothermal vents.

There are milk banks; I offer to donate.

Then the discovery: the maternal body is polluted. The medications I take for my anxiety and depression quirk the milk to a dangerous place—the donation center takes milk for preemies and other at-risk children. It is sold at $3.50 an ounce. Is this why they call it liquid gold?

Mine fills pipes.

I'm led to a night where I slit each bag open—they clack against one another as they unfreeze—and fill the sink. Hundreds of ounces, because who needs all of that extra, when you are a mermaid?

I begin to write another book. I lactate from one manuscript to the next.

❀

And here, another way a mother is dismembered. Women at night, creeping downstairs to disgorge. Women in cubes with the *whuh whuh whuh* of mechanical sucking. The required kneading. To *dis*embody: to offer the bulb of bottled milk.

My daughter never took to the bottle, no matter how many night classes she'd screech through. My husband with his infinite tolerance; I'd drive home with stones beneath my chest, nipples slowly ceding to land. She'd jam fuzz and fripperies into her mouth, but he had to squirt milk into the squall in hopes some would stick.

My son will suck anything presented, any neat nipple. But I've been long at-home, so his bottle line-up is just pleasure, like his father's beer. He lets either of us lock his eyes; he's not so picky.

❀

At once I want to taste it. And never.

I remember a friend offering me a taste of her own milk, wiggling that little bottle in her hand. I declined.

But my curiosity brings me to taste my own: overly sweet, thick.

Chef Daniel Angerer of Klee Brasserie in Chelsea makes cheese from his wife's breastmilk. Canapé of breast-milk cheese with figs and Hungarian pepper. The flavor depends on the diet of the milk host.

When I shucked the bags I couldn't use, my hands smelled like spoiled milk for days. Awful smell, that. Even now, I am averse to the yeasty smell of breast pads.

A nest unfettered by feathers.

The citizens of the ancient Greek city of Ephesus spent 220 years constructing a temple dedicated to Diana/Artemis and is one of the Seven Wonders of the Ancient World.

The site was built and destroyed, built and destroyed. By mob, by earthquake, by fire.

Many images from this time remain—that of Artemis-of-many-breasts. On coins, she rests upon snakes or the ouroboroi, the snake eternally devouring itself. There is a variation on the statue with two-dozen smoothed-over breasts resembling eggs in a honeycomb.

I lick and lick my fingers.

❀

And then there is this: nearly two years after I found myself pregnant with my daughter, I menstruate. On my own: twenty-four hours of the brownest, saddest blood, but blood nonetheless. I bluster into the bedroom, where my husband is reading to our daughter. I am nearly as excited as I was when I waved the positive-pregnant-stick in his face in the middle of the night. He looks appropriately bewildered, and I giddily open a dusty box of Tampons.

I find myself in the doctor's office. We are preparing to try again.

This is where it gets confusing: because it wasn't a flourishing menstruation, the doctor opts for medication. I menstruate, but have shown no evidence of ovulation. She makes my calendar again, my head swims, I walk away with a slip of paper that confesses me back to drugs. I pick them up and stare them down on the countertop.

And when the medication doesn't prompt a bleed again, I worry. I pace and I wait and five days after the cycle should have started again, I take a pregnancy test.

I am pregnant again.

I have gotten pregnant. Naturally.

Cetacea: *The order of marine mammals that include dolphins, porpoises, and whales.*

I believe I epitomize

lumber

at my acupuncture appointment today. My sciatic nerve

is furious, bleating out small shards of pain.

The doctor said, *You must be one of those women who get as big as a garage.*
　　　　　It's an interesting image: baby-as-car,
　　　　　　　　　　humming until winter-warm.

But I prefer W H A L E ,

　　as it forgives my all-over　　enormity, allows me
to feel a bit peaceful,　　imagining myself as enclosed in
water too.

　　That word: *obese*.　　　A hook to hang me on.
　　　(Obeisance) (Obedient) (Obliging)

The doctor does what he does,

moving his work-chapped hands along my bare back,
stopping to punch me with his little contraption.

It isn't enough that he left me bee-stung,   so many needles,
but I'd pressed my stomach and breasts into any space
left for my lungs

and here goes the table with its   lift and fall lift and fall.

I want, again, to try for the mythical vaginal birth. I begin making my way through piles of snow to Rochester, Minnesota, traveling across stubbled fields, fallow after corn, through woods and single lanes, lonely traffic lights. I am reaching out to Mayo Clinic; somehow I am nestled on the conveyer belt. Is it instinct that sends me there, to polished metal and white walls, instead of the holy hum of a birthing center?

I'm hoping for a VBAC. Vaginal Birth After Caesarean. I am inspected. We spend my daughter's second birthday walking from room to room: I am ultrasounded, I am ungrounded, I am found small and wanting. Strange to be too small for anything when I feel so large. It takes a few appointments, and the story is more convoluted than I am telling it, but gradually, the doctors tell me there will be no induction, there will be no vaginal birth. Perhaps they should have installed a zipper.

It is Friday. I wait the whole of the weekend for my scheduled C-section on Monday. My husband takes me to Bodies: The Exhibition, which is somehow here again, on tour, and I start at the ghost-babies, the women whose bodies are stripped and waxed and held in place.

I cry. In the underground Habitrail of the Mayo Clinic, I snort and hold up my chin, so my lips fill with saltwater, but the mourning is brief. I am shocked and quiet, but by the time we reach the elevator, I have stopped crying, and by the time we come home, I take a nap.

They wheel me into the operating room at eight o'clock. At eight-fourteen, my son is born.

Do you want your tubes tied? No.
    Do you want your tubes
       tied? No.   *Do you want*
          your tubes tied?

Long, slow shake of the head. No. Why should I have to discuss this, tell this doctor what was already decided, that my hormones have been through *enough already* and if a third were to break through that poly-cystic ovary barrier, without even the discussion of drugs or treatments or my thighs whipped up into the air, it would be welcome. I know, *We're already in there, may as well,* but cease. I want no more altercations.

The doctor looks to my husband: *I tried, man.*

I hear that nervous laugh, he does not know what else to do, but in the car, he says, *I just wanted to say, Give it up, man.*

We protect each other this way, in our quiet; who wants to make the man who will wield the knife upset? Let him root out the babe and be gone. Leave me with a long open mouth, the one countering the pucker-shut of my cervix, sew me with sutures and glue and walk out of the room, doctor shedding his gloves, walk away with my placenta nested in a stainless steel bowl and my baby headed to examination.

My husband holding our son's hand, telling him how
beautiful he is, how welcome he is, how to never push

Mommy into anything, because
        instead of quiet,
                she roared him into the world.

    ⊛

I've always loved the caesura. I've loved the line-break, the use of white-space.

The caesura makes me think of: breath, feathers in fields, the down in nests, flight, drifting clouds, fog, ice crystals on windowpanes in winter, children lifting their arms while swinging or riding a bicycle (*no hands!*), the coast, sea oats, lungs.

When I was three years old, I was diagnosed with Kawasaki's Disease. My parents were afraid I might die; my mother slept each of the ten nights on an orange plastic cushion. When my grandparents came to visit, I was walking down the hallway with an IV. Everyone was crying. My grandparents were shocked at my frailty. My parents were thrilling at my learning to walk again.

It's not that I had forgotten, or even had therapy, but my joints had swollen so I could not get out of bed. My tongue resembled the texture of a strawberry.

—

After my daughter's birth, again, I could not walk. I lean into my husband like a doll. It takes agonizing time to go from bed to bathroom, even worse to sit, the worst to rise. When I am alone in the room with my daughter, I develop a fever. I cannot reach the nurse call button, do not realize there is one built into the bed. I am shaking so hard, I can hear the plastic of the armrests rattling.

Three days after I am released, I return. The doctor tells me, *I could open this right back up, if you wanted.* She's teasing. My husband, who braced my torso as I received my epidural and photographed the birth, cringes in the doorway. I am afraid. I still have trouble walking; my feet are so swollen I wear his slippers to the door.

—

After my son's birth, I beg them to remove the catheter. I do not even have to pee, but I force myself there anyway. I cannot be tethered to this bed. I develop hives all along my backside; I become a burning red welt.

The first night of my son's life, he rests. The second and the third, he nurses. For six hours. The nurses tell about me at shift change: I am the Nursing Mother. Lactation consultants lean in, guide my hand, run fingers along his throat, as if to say, *See this. This is what your bodies can do*. My head bobs and listens to the slick sound of his jaw pumping colostrum.

We call him Finnegan. Finn, the boyfish.

It takes me a few days, but eventually, I am able to look at the photographs of my son's birth. My husband does not hold back; I've asked for this. There's the placenta and all of its veins. And one pale-pink meaty something in the hands of a blue-gowned ghost. This? This is my uterus, being sewn together.

I have it, this twice shorn scar, purpled, slick. I keep it like a tattoo. The screaming stretch marks too, silverfish, running down my abdomen. I runnel my fingers along, like marbles.

After each birth, I lose more feeling in a strip of abdomen just above their leaving-place. One could tattoo these words there; I wouldn't feel a thing. And, too: I'd feel everything.

—

On the day before my son's due date, Rep. Mary Sue McClurkin states in an interview, "When a physician removes a child from a woman, that is the largest organ in a body. That's a big thing. That's a big surgery. You don't have any other organs in your body that are bigger than that."

—

According to the body's calendar, the intestines are the first organ of the human body to deteriorate after death. The uterus is the last.

—

When I sleep next to him, my skin traces his.

A year after my daughter was born, an ad campaign was launched on Milwaukee's city billboards featuring fat babies sleeping on polyp-ed beds: downy pillows, ruched sheets. One baby sleeps stomach-down; the ruddy-cheeked second sleeps at an angle. Each has a glinting knife, butcher-quality, slit under a pillow. The tagline: *Your baby sleeping with you can be just as dangerous.*

Maya sleeps between us, a wedge of a girl, sometimes planting a sweaty fist in an eye socket, sometimes knobbing bruises. Bedtime becomes a way to add fault lines, furrow a sheet.

I try to avert my eyes, but I cannot help the rabbit hole of stories: the nurse who smothered her child with her nursing breast, the drunk father who crushed his son on the sofa, the rotten words scrolling into my bedroom.

I pinch myself: *stay awake.* I contort myself, flayed: *circle around her.*

Now, there's four-in-a-bed: him, her, me, him. Bookended, I am. In hotels, I construct pillow fortresses, but my crooked arm never deviates; it's a permanent sleep-state. When I nap alone, I try to relish the freedom of position, but I just wake sore, my breasts knock-upon hard, my arms achy. I'm unhibernated and growlish. Bring him back, my little pinner-of-souls.

My elbow cocked in the air, my two-month-old son is nursing so enthusiastically, I wonder if my aureole will be sucked through to the bottom of his throat.

But it isn't enough. Despite my son's best efforts to relieve me of my breast, I have, over half-night, leaked and converted my bra to the slick, heavy consistency of a bath mat. As I write this, I am topless on my living room floor, one of my son's size one diapers bound to one breast, the other making loud snicking noises as the mechanical pump extracts the milk. I lose ten liquid ounces this way, pocketing them in plastic freezer bags that accumulate like dandelions. The sun is rising, rendering streetlamps obsolete.

This, my liquid gold. It's hard to feel this way—valuable— as I listen to my daughter wail upstairs; I have disrupted the family bed. I feel selfish—all three are waiting for my return. What if I stayed down to write this, or, better yet, what if I walked out that door, into the streetlight, naked as I am?

But this isn't all true. It's not just the breasts that are sublime. I carried them, kettledrum lit. I listen to the want in her voice: *Mom-eee, Mom-eee.* When so much else is gone, my uterus will stay, a pink sewn purse. This is how I basketed my heart.

I whisper back: *I carried you, deep into winter.*

Upstairs, I take our baby, warm as an organ. He goes to work again, pulling long and peaceful.

This tunnel is my home. Eye-locked, wintered-in.

We build a fire to keep the melt. My body warms to theirs; I am no longer the tinder but the fire itself. Our quartet, a little furnace of love.

We are brought bread and honey, our tongues expanding in our throat.

She'd pink in pleasure at the sight of our limb-woven home. Hestia, full of blessings. I've filled my arms with them.

Oh glory, I hymn to you.

qtd. in Baker, Katie JM. "Genius Alabama Rep. says a baby is the 'largest organ in a body.'" *Jezebel*. February 2013.

Bruijn, Melissa with Debby Gould. "Encouraging Worlds, Unintentional Harm." *Pathways to Family Wellness*. December 2010.

Conoley, Gillian. "Language and the Gaze at the Other," *The Grand Permission*, 207.

Dericotte, Toi. "Writing Natural Birth," *The Grand Permission*, 49.

Lachlan Cartwright and Jeremy Olshan. "Wife's baby milk in chef's cheese recipe." *New York Post*. March 2010.

Roy, Camille. "My Motherhood," *The Grand Permission*, 34.

van Dongen, Pieter WJ. "Caesarean section: etymology and early history." *South African Journal of Obstetrics and Gynaecology*. August 2009.

BOOKS

Fennelly, Beth Ann. *Great With Child*. 123.

Lispector, Clarice. *The Stream of Life*. (Quotes on pg. 23)

Miller, Leslie Adrienne. *The Resurrection Trade*.

Ogden, Daniel. *Magic, Witchcraft, and Ghosts in the Greek and Roman Worlds: A Sourcebook*.

Olds, Sharon. *Satan Says*.

Olds, Sharon. *The Gold Cell*.

Wolf, Naomi. *Misconceptions*, 136-137.

INTERNETS

http://www.wicca-spirituality.com/drawing-down-the-moon.html

http://paganwiccan.about.com/od/wiccanandpaganrituals/ht/
Draw_Down.html

http://www.usashaolintemple.org/chanbuddhism-history/

http://io9.com/the-creepiest-headless-portraits-from-the-victo-
rian-era

http://www.dailymail.co.uk/femail/article-407073/Fatally-
injured-mother-kept-alive-birth.html

http://articles.chicagotribune.com/1988-01-04news
/8803190627_1_extensive-brain-damage-baby-alive

http://www.guardian.co.uk/world/1999/dec/12/theobserver1

http://usatoday30.usatoday.com/news/nation/2005-06-15-sav-
ing-baby-cover_x.htm

http://the.honoluluadvertiser.com/article/2005/Dec/01/ln/
FP512010336.html

http://www.huffingtonpost.com/2012/04/23/nicholas-and-alex-
ander-bolden_n_1446588.html

http://www.menlo.com/folks/davis/Maya_Web/Maya_Name.
html

http://www.theoi.com/Heroine/Kallisto.html

http://kepler.nasa.gov/multimedia/Audio/sonification/

http://www.huffingtonpost.com/2012/08/21/the-sound-of-a-dying-star_n_1812314.html

http://consciousmovements.com/the-sound-of-becoming-a-mother/

http://www.nlm.nih.gov/exhibition/cesarean/part1.html

http://www.exploreforensics.co.uk/the-rate-of-decay-in-a-corpse.html

http://www.mythencyclopedia.com/Cr-Dr/Diana.html

http://dsc.discovery.com/tv-shows/gold-rush/about-this-show/gold-rush-mining-lexicon.htm

http://www.americancatholic.org/Messenger/May2006/Feature2.asp

http://www.jsonline.com/news/milwaukee/milwaukee-cosleeping-ad-stirs-nationwide-debate-4m33572-133987863.html

Thank you to the editors of the following publications who printed some of these pieces, at times in different form:

> *27 rue des fleures*
> *Anatomy & Etymology*
> *City of Bears* (chapbook, dancing girl press)
> *The New Megaphone*
> *Tupelo Press's 30/30 Project* (April 2013)
> *Whole Beast Rag*

Thank you to those who read and gave feedback on early versions of this book, including Joelle Biele, Éireann Lorsung, and Marcela Sulak. Great appreciation and debt goes to my fellow members of the Caldera Poetry Collective: Meryl DePasquale, Opal C McCarthy, and Colleen Coyne. Thanks to *Surge: An Oral Poetics* (Eohippus Labs Tract Series) for inspiring this book. To the good people at the Loft, especially Jerod Santek and Jude Nutter, as well as Kelly Hansen Maher, MaryAnn Franta Moenck, and Paige Riehl for their insights. Great appreciation goes to my writing group in St. Paul, especially to Brett Elizabeth Jenkins, hostess extraordinaire, and Katharine Rauk for her words. Thank you to Arielle Greenberg, Sarah Vap, and the rest of the [Poet Moms], and to my generous editors, Diana Arterian and Fox Henry Frazier.

Thank you to: my parents, his parents, my sisters (both by blood and by heart): Chelsea, Kelly, and Emily. And especially, thank you to Ryan, Maya, and Finnegan: you continue to be every beautiful thing I've ever wanted to write.

Molly Sutton Kiefer is the author of the poetry chapbooks *City of Bears* (dancing girl press, 2013) and *The Recent History of Middle Sand Lake* (Astounding Beauty Ruffian Press, 2010). She is poetry editor for *Midway Journal* and runs *Balancing the Tide: Motherhood and the Arts | An Interview Project*. She lives in Minnesota with her family. More can be found at www.mollysuttonkiefer.com.

PHOTO: RYAN KIEFER